# THE Magic OF sisters

*Written and Compiled by Laurie Kay*

Sisterhood is a special bond that is enduring and rewarding. In writing this book, people from many walks of life shared with me things that make a sister special. These shared memories are important to all of us because they remind us that even the simplest things we say or do can have a powerful and lifelong impact on those we love.

In this book you will find a variety of memories, shared by many. You will discover that these — and your own inspirational memories — truly reveal the magic that is... The Magic of Sisters.

*This book is dedicated* *to my* *Sister*

*After I graduated from high school, I struggled with the decision whether to attend college or not because I just didn't have the money. My sister encouraged me to enroll in school and loaned me the money to get started. Because of her support, I got my degree and have enjoyed a successful professional career (which, by the way, has allowed me to more than pay her back).*

- Susan

My sister and I are best friends. Every year we take a "*sister trip*" together. It doesn't have to be a fancy trip; we just love spending time together laughing and enjoying each other's company.

- Beth

Although my sister lived several states away,

she helped me through a very difficult

divorce. She sent cards just to let

me know she was thinking about me and called

from time to time to see how I was doing and

to let me know she cared. I could not have

gotten through it without her.

- Deb

I was having a difficult time dealing with the death of my dog, Ginger, who was my friend and companion for twelve years. To *ease my struggle,* my sister made me a beautiful scrapbook containing photos and funny, memorable stories about my years with Ginger.

I couldn't ask for a better sister.

- Sandra

My sister's *joyful laughter* keeps everyone in high spirits. When she laughs, we can't help but laugh along with her.

- Becky

My sister always gave me beautiful gifts that she made herself. They were particularly special because she made them *from her heart* and with me in mind.

- Reggie

My older sister made me feel special when she had a

birthday slumber party at our house with of some

her friends. Even though I was the "little" sister, she

## included me in her slumber

party with her friends instead of leaving me out.

- Connie

My sister is a *unique gift* to me.
She listens... makes me laugh... does things
with me... and is someone I trust and can
talk to about anything.

- Joyce

My sis has *touched my life*

in special ways — we work together in business...

laugh together... cry together... and help

each other out in any way we can.

- Charlene

*The* day my older sister left home to begin a

new job overseas, she presented me with a small

box. I couldn't imagine what was in the box,

but was unbelievably surprised when I opened it

to discover the keys to her red Mustang convertible!

She was giving me her car since she was going

away! What a wonderful sister!

- Julie

When I was in high school, I earned a leading role in a school play, which was a dream come true for me. On opening night, I was astounded to see my sister in the audience. It was a *special surprise* because she had driven two days to be at my performance!

- Bill

I was a chain-smoker for many years. When I finally decided to quit, my sister *stood* *by me* and encouraged me. I haven't had a cigarette in ten years and I thank her for giving me the extra support I needed to improve my health and life.

- Andrew

When my older sister and I were in high school, she let me wear her cute clothes. Now that I have two teenage daughters of my own, I realize that her generosity was an example of true

## "sisterly love!"

- Melissa

For my 13th birthday, my older sister gave me a "make-up" birthday party. We invited all my girlfriends to the party and my sister and her friend provided the make-up. We spent hours putting make-up on each other—laughing and talking the whole time. It was the best birthday party I ever had!

- Gina

*I consider myself somewhat of a loner and*

*don't keep in contact with too many people,*

*but always on my birthday, my sister faithfully calls*

*me. Usually when she calls I don't even remember*

*that it is my birthday. I really appreciate her*

## thoughtful effort.

*- Robert*

My only sister is mentally challenged and lives in

a group home. When I visit her she makes me

# feel special because she excitedly

runs to hug me, shouting to her friends,

"My sister is here! My sister is here!"

- Karen

As a young father, I suddenly found myself in a

situation of having to raise my two daughters alone.

Fortunately, my three sisters became very involved

in my daughters' lives and now my girls feel they

have **been blessed** with

three wonderful mothers!

-Tad

My two sisters and I get together for a special

"sister's reunion" every year. Each year we travel to

a different location to meet, have fun and just

# spend time together.

One year, we met (appropriately so) in Sisters,

Oregon for our sister's reunion.

- Evelyn

*When my doctor told me that I had a health problem that required me to be in a care center for several days, my sister supported me by getting on an airplane and traveling to my home to take care of my children. Having my children entrusted to her care relieved me of great stress and I can never thank her enough for her generosity in doing that for me and my family.*

- Cheryl

My sister and I have a special relationship. We
*share everything* with each
other: laughter, tears, phone calls, emails, shopping,

movies, lunches, dinners, and late night talks.

All these things create a special bond

that's unique to us.

- Catherine

My little sister means a lot to me. She has

been supportive when I've struggled with

financial and marital hardship. When things

get tough, she is there to encourage me and do

## whatever it takes

to help me get through it.

- Brad

Even though I travel a lot,

my sister makes me feel special because

## she is thoughtful

and makes a concerted effort to keep in touch.

- Jan

I just *love my sister* because

she tells me the truth when I need to hear it

and helps me see things as they really are —

not as I think they are.

- Jerrold

For our 40th wedding anniversary, my youngest sister handmade for my husband and me a special memory quilt depicting our years together. The fact that my sister would do that for us — even though she worked full time — made me feel

# extremely special.

- Iva Jean

My sis is absolutely the best because she has proven over the years that she would *do* *anything* for me.

- Beth

My sister shares my love for movies. Our husbands

support our outings and stay home with the kids so

we can enjoy a good movie and spend some fun

"*sister time*" together.

- Jeannie

As a young girl, I used to sit on the bed and watch

my oldest sister put on her makeup. When she saw

how fascinated I was with the whole process,

she sat down and put makeup on me as well.

As a result of her sisterly

love, I felt as beautiful as she!

- Virginia

*My sister has always been very gentle, kind, thoughtful and caring. She always makes or buys me little things that she thinks I might like and we laugh a lot when we're together. She is my little sister, but when we're together, I try to tell everyone that she's the older one and I am the younger one — however, it usually doesn't work.*

- Nancy

Even though our families and careers have taken us on different paths, my sister and I have managed to maintain *a special bond* and be there for each other when needed.

- Jack

No matter what I need to talk about, my sis is there

to listen, support and encourage me.

- Charlotte

My sister has always *been there for me,* listens to me when I have problems, and helps me with honest advice when I ask for it.

- Roy

I have a special relationship with my sister-in-law because I can talk to her about anything. I can talk to her about things that I may not want to discuss with other family members and she always seems to understand.

- Joye

For many years, my sister and I followed our own paths and weren't very close. Since the death of our mother, we have created a new bond and found a new closeness that we didn't have before. We *sincerely care* about each other and are there for one another, no matter what.

- Judy

The thing that is so special about my sister is that she *gives unselfishly* and doesn't expect anything in return.

- Marie

My sister is *my confidant* and I can talk to her about anything. It is comforting to share the joys and problems in our lives and I know she will always be there for me.

- Viv

Growing up in Canada, my sister and I would take

"pin-up pictures" of each other. That means we

would look at the girls on the pin-up calendars and

try to dress up and pose just like them. We would

laugh and *have great fun*

taking pictures of each other and posing

for the camera!

- Lenore

*When* my sisters and I were very young,

we lost our mother and had to take care of each

other. We are very close and even though we all

have our own families now, we continue to

help one another and we are always there

to support each other whatever the need.

- Maria

My sister and I are very close. We

guide and help each
other through the hard times in life.

- Mandy

My sister and I do a lot together. She made me

feel really special when she gave me a

## wonderful treat — a trip to

Las Vegas — with all expenses paid!

I think she's just the best sister!

- Irene

On occasion, when Mom and Dad went on a date to the movies, my sister would babysit my brother and me. This was always a *fun time* because she made it special by pretending we were spending an evening at the movies too. She would play a videotape movie, make popcorn, and let us act out our own "real life" commercials during intermission.

- Donald

My sister and I are different in personality, but **totally support each other** in every way. We are only a phone call from each other whenever we need help.

- Miriam

With my birthday being the day after Christmas,

it is often "lost" in the Christmas festivities.

On my 50th birthday, however, my younger sister

made me feel special when she made an

# extra effort to acknowledge me by

planning a special birthday celebration just for me.

- Evanne

I can talk to my sister about

*anything and* **she listens**

*without judging or criticizing me.*

- Joan

My sister and I are really close. She makes me feel

special because I have no children of my own and

over the years she has generously let me be a

# part of her family

and share in the lives of her children.

- Loretta

We are identical twins and have been very close all

our lives. We are rarely apart and when we are, it

feels like a part of us is missing. What's more, we

share everything... *what's mine*

*is hers,* no questions asked!

- Patti and Matti

*Because* my children were my first priority, I didn't have much time to pamper myself after my second child was born (just nineteen months after my first). Realizing this, my sister surprised me one day by arranging care for my children then taking me to a spa for a massage, manicure and pedicure. It was a special afternoon of fun and pampering and because of her thoughtfulness I felt renewed!

- Dawn

I have an "adopted" sister. Even though she is not

my sister by blood, she has always been there for me,

# helping me through
# the worst days of my life and

sharing the good days with me as well. Her

generosity will never leave my heart.

- Ann

When my life feels overwhelming, I can always count

on the help of my sister. She hugs me when I need it.

She helps me laugh at my own shortcomings and

# lifts my spirits on days that

test my patience and fortitude.

- Olivia

My sister is someone I can trust and who can make me feel better

when it seems that life is just too much to handle!

- Joanie

My sister is *my best friend.*

We laugh together, cry together, encourage each

other, and comfort each other. We are always there

for each other spiritually and emotionally even when

we're physically apart.

- Faith

I am close with all my sisters — they are

always there for me — but I have an especially

# close bond with my younger sister. I

trust her and can talk to her about anything

and feel comfortable about it.

- Veronica

# My sister is the best

*because she was willing to loan me money*

*when I was in a difficult financial situation.*

*- Mary*

# Sisters are great! All my

sisters make me feel special because they are

always there for me and I am there for them...

no matter the circumstances.

- Kathy

*My sister makes me feel*

*special because she totally*

# *spoils me!*

*- Sophie*

*If this book has touched you and you would like to share*
*with us a memory of your own, please email us at*
**memory@magicof.com**

© 2005 Havoc Publishing
San Diego, California
U.S.A.

Text by Laurie Kay

ISBN 0-7416-1325-5

www.havocpub.com

Made in China